D0246257

# All New Dad Jokes

An Hachette UK Company
www.hachette.co.uk

First published in Great Britain in 2019 by Cassell, an imprint of
Octopus Publishing Group Ltd
Carmelite House
50 Victoria Embankment
London EC4Y 0DZ
www.octopusbooks.co.uk

Distributed in the US by
Hachette Book Group
1290 Avenue of the Americas
4th and 5th Floors
New York, NY 10104

Distributed in Canada by
Canadian Manda Group
664 Annette St.
Toronto, Ontario, Canada M6S 2C8

ISBN 978 1 78840 174 6

A CIP catalogue record for this book is available from the British Library.

Printed and bound in the United Kingdom.

13

Publishing Director Stephanie Jackson
Editorial Assistant Cara Armstrong
Designer Jack Storey
Typesetter Penny Stock
Production Controller Grace O'Byrne

# All New Dad Jokes

**– From the Instagram sensation –**
**@DadSaysJokes**

Dedicated to Grandad Browning,
an endless repository of Dad Jokes

# Introduction

@DadSaysJokes is back.

A year after we published our first volume of the cheesiest jokes this side of Cheeseville, here's our second edition. Be warned – this time round the jokes are full groan!

But seriously folks...We couldn't have done this without our growing band of dedicated followers. Together we've made the world laugh. Kit, my son and the creator of @DadSaysJokes, continues to rely on me to make the world a jollier place – and that's what I've tried to do with this new book.

Enjoy and keep the jokes coming.

Kit & Andrew

I don't understand why no one likes the Night King on *Game of Thrones*.

I think he looks pretty chilled.

---

What is made out of brass and sounds like Tom Jones?

Trombones.

Son: What exactly is an acorn?

Father: Well, in a nutshell it's an oak tree.

The man who invented auto-correct has died.

His funfair is on sundial at moon.

———————————

My least favourite colour is purple.

I dislike it more than red and blue combined.

My wife just accused me of having zero empathy.

I just don't understand why she feels that way.

———————

Did you know that diarrhoea is hereditary?

It runs in your jeans.

A kid decides to burn his house down.

Dad – putting his arm round his wife, both with tears welling in their eyes – "That's arson."

———————

A Roman walks into a bar, holds up two fingers and says, "I'll have five beers please."

How did the hipster burn his tongue?

He ate his food before it was cool.

**What is a Jehovah's Witness' favourite band?**

**The Doors.**

---

**I woke up this morning to find that someone had dumped a load of Lego bricks on my doorstep.**

**I don't know what to make of it.**

What's the difference between Dubai and Abu Dhabi? The people in Dubai don't like *The Flintstones*, but the people in Abu Dhabi do.

———————

I just learned the medical name for Viagra.

Mycoxaflopin.

Officer: I'm sorry to say, sir, but it looks like your wife has been hit by a bus.

Man: Yeah, but she's got a great personality.

I just saw a real idiot at the gym.

He put a water bottle in the Pringles holder on the treadmill.

———————

So I stopped at this roadside stand that said lobster tails £2.

I paid my £2 and the stallholder said, "Once upon a time there was this lobster..."

Nine months isn't really that long.

It just feels like a maternity.

———————

If you rearrange the letters
of POSTMEN...

They become VERY ANGRY.

I asked my wife how to turn Alexa off.

She said, "How about walking through the room naked?"

———

I'm reading a great book about Lubricants.

It's non-friction.

To the man who
invented zero:

Thanks for nothing.

I once ate a dictionary.

It gave me thesaurus throat I've ever had.

_____

I can't take my dog to the pond anymore because the ducks keep attacking him.

Guess that's what I get for buying a pure bread dog.

I went to the doctor to tell her of my dreams about Tom Jones...

Patient: Is this common?

Doctor: It's not unusual...

I went to a haunted bed and breakfast
in France.

The place was giving me the crêpes.

———————

I've just written a book about falling
down a staircase.

It's a step-by-step guide.

**WHAT DO WE WANT!!??**

**RACING CAR NOISES!!!**

**WHEN DO WE WANT THEM!!??**

**Neeeeoooooooooowwwwww!!!!!!**

---

**Why did the French football team keep scoring own goals?**

**Toulouse.**

I think I've eaten some bad seafood.

I'm feeling a little eel.

_____

I used to know a guy who
did circumcisions.

The money wasn't great, but he got to
keep the tips.

What do you call a man who pours
a lot of drinks?

Phil.

----

My wife left me because of my
obsession with walkie talkies, saying,
"It's over."

I replied, "It's what? Over."

My wife hated my impulse purchase of a revolving chair. But then she sat in it.

Eventually she came around.

———————

The first picture of a black hole has been released.

It sucks.

**What do you call an elephant who doesn't matter?**

**An irrelephant.**

_____

**I met a Buddhist monk who refused anaesthetic during his root canal surgery.**

**His aim? Transcend dental medication.**

# How does Darth Vader like his toast?

# On the dark side.

**What happened when 30 got hungry?**

**38.**

_____

**My wife threatened to leave me because of my "filthy and disgusting habits".**

**I was so shocked I nearly choked on my toenails.**

**What do you call a guy with kids in Holland?**

**An Amsterdad.**

---

**What's blue and smells like red paint?**

**Blue paint.**

How do you spot a blind man at a nudist beach?

It's not hard...

_____

I showed up at the weekly kleptomaniac anonymous meeting.

But all the seats were already taken.

Officer: I'm arresting you for downloading everything on Wikipedia.

Suspect: No wait! I can explain everything!

The shortest sentence is "I am."

The longest sentence is "I do."

————————

I'm friends with 25 letters of the alphabet.

I don't know y.

My friend recently quit his job to pursue a career in miming.

I haven't heard from him since.

———————

What did sushi A say to sushi B when they met.

Wasabi.

What do you call a fly without wings?

A walk.

How do you know how heavy a chilli pepper is?

Give it a weigh, give a weigh, give it a weigh now.

_____

A storm blew away 25% of my roof last night.

Oof.

I hate people with missing toes.

Because I'm lack toes intolerant.

---

What's the difference between me and a calendar?

A calendar has dates.

Why did the invisible man turn down the job?

Because he couldn't see himself doing it.

———————

Four fonts walk into a bar. The barman says, "We don't want your type in here."

Man: I'm here to dispute 60 of my parking tickets.

Judge: Repeat infractions.

Man: OK. I'm here to dispute ⅗ of my parking tickets.

**How do you make a water bed more bouncy?**

**Add spring water.**

_____

**My wife gets angry that I keep introducing her as my ex-girlfriend.**

I just spotted an albino Dalmatian.

It was the least I could do to help.

————————

I have a playlist of songs from Eminem, the Cranberries and the Peanuts.

I named it the Trail Mix.

I've just downloaded the Queen movie, *Bohemian Rhapsody*.

I think it was filmed in a cinema though as I see a little silhouetto of a man...

---

I ordered a chicken and an egg online.

...I'll let you know.

My dad was bragging about his hearing aid...

Dad: State of the art, cost me a fortune.

Son: Awesome, what type is it?

Dad: 2:30

How does it feel
when you cross
a melon with a
cauliflower?

Melancholy.

After an unsuccessful harvest, why did the farmer decide to try a career in music?

Because he had a ton of sick beets.

---

I grew facial hair without telling anyone?

It's my secret 'stache.

It's probably not safe for me to be driving right now.

But, hey, bad brakes have never stopped me before.

———————

I sat next to a baby for a 10 hour flight. I didn't think it was possible for someone to scream for 10 hours straight.

Even the baby was impressed I pulled it off.

Man one: A cannibal once took my sister to see a Russell Crowe movie.

Man two: *Gladiator*?

Man one: No I really miss her.

I went to the bar with a boxer, but he's just a lightweight.

———

I've been watering my herbs with leftover coffee.

I love coffee thyme.

My dad said I always loved alphabet soup when I was young.

But it was just him putting words in my mouth .

———————

No bragging, but I made six figures last year.

So they named me the worst employee at the toy factory.

Dad: Find a girl with an embarrassing tattoo and try to convince her to marry you.

Son: Why?

Dad: She knows how to make bad decisions, but is prepared to stick by them.

# Why can't you breed an eel with an eagle?

# It's eeleagle.

I took the shell off my racing snail
thinking it would make him go faster.

But instead he's now more sluggish.

———————

Working out is like a drug to me.

I don't do drugs.

I went into a lingerie store and asked the assistant if the underwear was satin.

"No!" she said. "It's brand new."

———————

What does an unhappy Scandinavian say?

I wish I was never Björn.

I taught my daughter what a bargain meant.

She said, "Thanks, Dad. That means a great deal!"

———————

Where do naughty rainbows go?

Prism.

I just said "no comment" all the way through the police interview.

I didn't get the job.

———————

My wife told me to stop making references to Bruce Willis movies.

I said,"Sorry, babe. Old habits die hard."

**The furniture store keeps calling me.**

**All I wanted was one nightstand!**

---

**Why do elephants drink?**

**To forget.**

I named my horse Mayo.

Mayo neighs.

_____

One day I changed a light bulb, crossed the road and walked into a bar.

Then I realized my whole life was a joke.

Interviewer: Your résumé says you take things too literally.

Me: When the hell did my résumé learn to talk?

The instructor in my self-defence class said that the most effective place to kick a man is near his knees.

Personally, I think it's nuts.

———————

I turned suddenly to my son and said, "Name two pronouns!"

He panicked and yelled back, "Who? Me?"

I told my boss I was tired of being a human cannonball.

So he fired me!

I asked my wife if I was the only one she'd been with.

She said yes, all the others had been nines and tens.

———————

A local barber in my neighbourhood was arrested for selling drugs.

Unbelievable – I'd been his customer for years and had no idea he was a barber.

I got fired from my job at the bank today.

An old lady asked me to check her balance – so I pushed her over.

———————

When is a car not a car?

When it turns into a driveway.

I was in a liqour store and the owner asked me, "Do you need help?"

I said, "Yes, but I'll have a bottle of whisky instead."

———————

Why do astronomers put beef in their shampoo?

For meatier showers.

I quit my job as a postman after the first letter they handed to me to deliver.

I looked at it and thought,
"This isn't for me."

––––––––––

My dad lost his job at the cemetery yesterday. He buried someone in the wrong plot.

It was a grave mistake.

My friend fell in a river in Egypt last week, but swears he didn't.

He's in de Nile.

———————

I'm American and I'm sick of people saying, "America is the stupidest country in the world."

Personally, I think Europe is the stupidest country in the world.

Have you heard of the blind
cyclop's brothers?

Neither have eye.

———————————

Here's the thing about cliff hangers...

I love telling
Dad jokes.

Sometimes
he laughs!

**A man walks into a chemist's and says...**

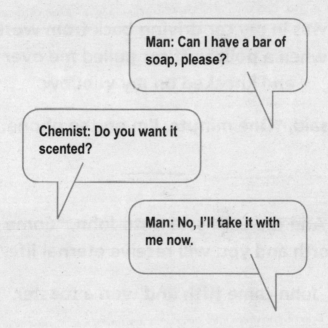

I was in my car driving back from work when a police officer pulled me over and knocked on my window.

I said, "One minute, I'm on the phone."

———————

And the Lord said unto John, "Come forth and you will receive eternal life."

John came fifth and won a toaster.

My wife accused me of being immature.

I told her to get out
of my fort immediately.

———————

I've been taking Viagra for my sunburn.

It doesn't cure it, but it keeps the sheets
off my legs.

My three favourite things are eating my family and not using commas.

---

Statistics say that one out of three people in a relationship is unfaithful.

I just need to work out if that's my wife or my girlfriend.

I was in a good mood till I started petting a duckling in the park.

Then I started feeling a little down.

———————

I've got a friend who reminds me of a software update.

Every time I see him I groan, "Not now."

My wife just put on her new dress and then told me to zip it.

I have no idea what I've done wrong. I didn't say anything!

---

When do people start using their trampolines more?

Spring time.

What do you call
a constipated detective?

No shit Sherlock.

———

Bro, can you pass me that leaflet?

Brochure.

My wife traumatically ripped the sheets off me last night.

I will recover

———————

I asked my grandmother how she is enjoying her new stairlift.

She said, "It's driving me up the wall."

I used to hate facial hair.

But then it grew on me.

A book just fell on my head.

I've only got my shelf to blame.

———————

A bus station is where a bus stops.
A train station is where a train stops.

On my desk, I have a work station.

Police have arrested the World Tongue Twister Champion.

They said he'll be given a tough sentence.

———————

It was a bleak day when we heard about the explosion down at the animal shelter...

It was raining cats and dogs!

**What do you call a wandering caveman?**

**A Meanderthal.**

_____

**What's blue and doesn't weigh
very much?**

**Light blue.**

I went trick or treating as Gandhi and kept all my candy in a hat. And when a guy tried to take the candy from my hat I said, "My hat my candy."

---

A girl came up to me and said she recognized me from a vegetarian restaurant.

I was a bit confused because I've never met herbivore.

What do you call a pit full of donkeys?

An asshole.

_____

As I suspected, someone has been adding soil to my garden.

The plot thickens.

**My mum wasn't happy with my school report...**

A warning to the person who stole my glasses.

I have contacts!

This morning I saw my neighbour talking to her cat; it was obvious the poor women thought the cat understood her.

When I got home I told my dog...we laughed a lot.

———————

There was a catastrophic cyber-attack recently; the government is still looking for the hacker.

I think he ran some ware.

My wife said, "It's over" and just walked out on me! But I just sat there.

I always like watching the credits to the end.

———————

I met a girl the other night at a club who said she'd show me a good time.

When we got outside she ran a 40-metre dash in just 4.5 seconds.

**What do you give a cannibal if he turns up late for your dinner party?**

**The cold shoulder.**

---

**What word has five letters, but becomes shorter when you add two more?**

**Short.**

My dad told me to stop pretending to be a farm animal.

He was sick of me horsing around.

———————

Why should you never iron a shamrock?

Because you shouldn't press your luck.

I tripped over my wife's bra.

It was a booby trap.

———————

My ex-wife cheated on me with her deaf best friend.

Honestly, I should have seen the signs.

What do you call a man with a flatfish on his head?

Ray.

———————

How does the Pope pay for things online?

He uses his Papal account.

What do you call a nervous witch?

A twitch.

———————

What do you call friends you like to eat with?

Taste buds.

My friends all claim I'm the cheapest person they've ever met.

I don't buy it!

———————

Every year St Patrick's day keeps on getting bigger.

I think it might even keep on Dublin.

Do you want to buy a broken barometer?

No pressure.

Some people have trouble sleeping...

But I can do it with my eyes closed.

_____

My boss hates it when I shorten his name to Dick.

Especially when his name is Steve.

I'm creating an app to find qualified electricians in your area.

It's called wattsapp.

———————

I was having trouble fastening my seatbelt...

And then it just clicked.

I just lost 20% of my couch.

Ouch.

———————

What do you call a mouse that swears?

A cursor.

I used to run a dating agency
for chickens.

But I was struggling to make hens meet.

———

I met a guy from Australia who works
in IT.

I asked, "Do you come from a LAN down
under?"

I'm the principal of a school called
St Richard's.

So I guess you could say
I'm the dickhead.

———————

In college I was so broke I couldn't
afford the electricity bill.

Those were the darkest days of my life.

Getting my toy drone stuck up in a tree wasn't the worst thing that happened to me today.

But it's up there.

_____

What is a sausage made up of annoying children?

A bratwurst.

What do you call a sad cup of coffee?

A depresso.

Just got back from a job interview where I was asked if I could perform under pressure.

I said I wasn't too sure about that, but I do a wicked "Bohemian Rhapsody".

---

Why did the chicken cross the playground?

To get to the other slide.

When you pull a pin from a grenade,
how do you put it back in?

Quick answers please!

_____

As I get older and remember all the
people I lost along the way, I think
to myself...

Maybe a career as a tour guide was not
the right choice.

After you die, what part of your body is the last to stop working?

Your pupils. They dilate.

————————

I hate it when my wife keeps telling me that "I don't get it."

What does it even mean?

**What do you call a donkey with three legs?**

**A wonkey.**

---

**What colour is the wind?**

**Blew.**

I've only just discovered you can now get Viagra tea bags. They don't improve your sex life...

But they stop your biscuits going soft.

———

What's Iron Man without his suit?

Stark Naked.

Boss: Send me one of those funny dad jokes.

Me: I can't, I'm busy working.

Boss: That's hilarious. Do you have any more?

Who is the coolest doctor in the hospital?

The hip consultant.

While most puns make me feel numb.

Maths puns make me feel number.

―――――

What do you call a murderer who only poisons your breakfast?

A cereal killer.

The man who invented Velcro died.

RIP.

---

If I had a wooden eye, I'd have a
wooden eye, wouldn't I ?

There are straight laws...and there are bylaws.

---

I blame Mother Earth for all earthquakes.

It's her fault.

I once accidentally bumped into Bono.

He got angry and said, "Don't push me coz I'm close to the Edge."

———————

Have you visited conjunctivitis.com?

It's a site for sore eyes.

My wife text messaged me with one word: "Earth."

It meant the world to me.

———————

I was diagnosed with a chronic fear of giants.

Feefiphobia.

**What did the doctor say to the man covered in cling film?**

**"I can clearly see you're nuts."**

---

**Why is a panda the most dangerous animal in the animal kingdom?**

**Because it eats shoots and leaves.**

**What happens when the smog lifts over Los Angeles?**

**UCLA.**

---

**Milk is the fastest liquid in the world.**

**It's pasteurized before you can see it.**

I think my wife is putting glue on my antique weapons' collection.

She denies it, but I'm sticking to my guns.

———————

I bought a pair of shoes from a drug dealer yesterday.

I don't know what he laced them with, but I've been tripping all day.

What should a
lawyer always wear
to court?

A good lawsuit.

Job interviewer: And where would you see yourself in five years' time, Mr Jeffries?

Me: Personally, I believe my biggest weakness is in listening.

What do you call a £1,000 door?

A grand entrance.

———

What did the fisherman say to
the magician?

Pick a cod, any cod.

**What's an optimistic vampire's favourite drink?**

**B-positive.**

———————

**How do you make a Swiss roll?**

**You push him over.**

My boss wouldn't stop making pancake jokes.

So I battered him.

_____

What do you call a funny mosquito?

Malarious!

If I ever find the doctor who screwed up my limb replacement surgery...

I'll kill him with my bear hands.

———————

My wife caught me cross-dressing and said it's over.

So I packed her clothes and left.

What do computers and air conditioners
have in common.

They both become useless once you
open windows.

———————

My friends laughed at me when I said
I had a hot date and they said
she was imaginary.

Well, the last laugh is on them because
they're imaginary too.

My wife complains
I don't buy
her flowers.

To be honest, I
didn't know she
sold flowers.

Does anyone know if you can take a skin graft from a donkey and transplant it onto a mate of mine who was burned?

Just ass skin for a friend.

———————

As my wife was preparing dinner I told her what a nice ham she had.

"But it would be a shame if you put an 's' at the front and 'e' at the end."

My wife and I had an argument about which vowel is the most useful.

I won.

_____

What do you call a man with no shins?

Tony.

**What do you call a horse that lives next door?**

**A neighbour.**

---

**I left my wife because she was obsessed with counting.**

**I wonder what she's up to now?**

I have a very good feeling about my job interview today. The manager said they were looking for somebody responsible.

"You've found your man," I replied, "whenever there was a problem in my last job, they always said that I was responsible!"

———————

I bought an impressionist painting of some flowers, but when I got back home the cat scratched it.

Now I'm trying to sell it as a Clawed Monet.

**What's the difference between a piano and a fish?**

**You can tune a piano but you can't tuna fish.**

———————

**I wonder what my parents did to fight boredom before the internet?**

**I asked my 18 brothers and sisters and they don't know either.**

My wife is furious at our next door neighbour who sunbathes nude in her garden.

Personally, I'm on the fence.

———————

What do you say when you tickle a tiny millionaire?

Gucci Gucci Gucci

**What do you call 52 pieces of bread?**

**A deck of carbs.**

_____

**What do you call a retired miner?**

**Doug.**

Why are ancient history lecturers boring?

They tend to Babylon.

I was wondering, why does a Frisbee appear larger the closer it gets?

Then it hit me.

_____

They all laughed when I said I wanted to be a comedian.

Well, they're not laughing now.

Time flies like an arrow.

Fruit flies like a banana.

———————

I told my wife she'd drawn her
eyebrows on too low.

She just sat and scowled at me.

Last week a German shepherd defecated in front of me on my lawn!

And yesterday he brought his dog along.

_____

People always ask me where I got my incredibly detailed tattoo done but never believe me when I tell them Spain.

Nobody expects the Spanish ink precision.

Yesterday my brother accidentally swallowed some weed killer.

Fortunately, he saw the fungicide.

---

Went to the doctor and said, "Have you got anything for wind?"

He gave me a kite.

I would like to be a millionaire just like my dad.

He always wanted to be a millionaire too.

---

What do you call a dentist's personal ship?

The tooth ferry.

This morning I tried to catch some fog.

Mist.

―――――――――

The guy who stole my diary just died.

My thoughts are with his family.

What does a panda use to
make pancakes?

A pan...duh!

_____

The internet is so dangerous! I searched
how to become an arsonist...

And immediately received
50,000 matches!

I just found out "AUGGHHH" isn't a real word.

I can't express how that makes me feel.

French people are so hardcore.

They eat pain for breakfast.

_____

I hate auto-correct, it always makes me say things I didn't Nintendo.

Job interviewer: In the beginning, you'll be earning £20,000, later on that can increase to £40,000.

Me: OK, I'll come again later then.

Someone threw a bottle of omega 3 pills at me.

Luckily my injuries were only super fish oil.

_____

What's the difference between a seagull and a baby without a nappy?

One flits across the shore...

My girlfriend and her family all say I'm paranoid.

At least I'm pretty sure that's what they're all saying behind my back.

———

My girlfriend said, "You act like a detective too much. I want to split up."

"Good idea," I replied. "We can cover more ground that way!"

**Can February March?**

**No, but April May.**

---

**People think being a waiter isn't a respectable job.**

**But, hey, it puts food on the table.**

What's the difference between an angry circus owner and a Roman barber?

One is a raving showman and the other is a shaving Roman.

---

People always told my dad that his pride would be the death of him...

And sure enough he was eaten by his favourite lion last Friday.

I once had a
conversation with
a dolphin.

We just clicked.

**Did you hear about the microphone checker that got really drunk?**

**He had one two one two one two many.**

---

**I went into an Apple store and farted. Everyone started glaring at me.**

**I said: "What? It's not my fault you don't have windows!"**

As soon as space travel is possible, I'm moving from the Milky Way to the Soymilky Way galaxy.

I'm galactose intolerant.

———————

I've just bought the personalized number plate BAA BAA.

For my black jeep.

Why is girlfriend one word, but best friend is two words?

Because your best friend gives you space when you need it.

———————

What do you call someone who drills holes?

Boring.

Police have warned of a man in craft stores dipping his testicles in glitter.

It's pretty nuts.

---

What starts with an "o" and ends with "nions" and sometimes make you cry?

Opinions.

A friend asked me," What rhymes with orange?"

I said, "No, it doesn't."

———————

I was drinking my milkshake on a cliff and thought:

Wow, this is ledge n dairy.

What word starts with "e", ends with "e", and only has one letter in it?

Envelope.

---

Gonorrhoea would have been a great name for diarrhoea medicine.

The oldest computer can be traced back
to Adam and Eve.

It was an Apple with extremely
limited memory. Just one byte. Then
everything crashed.

———————

I buy my guns from a guy called T-Rex.

He's a small arms dealer.

Juggling seems fun.

I just don't have the balls to do it.

Do you guys remember that "One Hit Wonder" Gotye guy?

You could say that he was somebody that we used to know.

———————

What was Beethoven's favourite snack?

BA-NA-NA-NA

**What did the German sausage say to his friend?**

**You are the wurst.**

_____

**Why is 68 afraid of 70?**

**Because 69 and 70 got into a fight and 71.**

I can't believe that viruses and bacteria would just invade my body without permission.

That makes me sick.

———————

My wife thinks I don't give her enough privacy.

At least that's what she said in her diary.

I went to the store to pick up eight cans of Sprite.

But when I got home I realized I'd only picked 7Up.

———

I hate the key E minor.

It gives me the E-B-G-Bs.

What did the black pepper say to his wife after coming out of the grinder?

Don't worry, I'm fine.

_____

I asked my friend Sam to sing a song about the iPhone.

And then Samsung.

Man: Boss, can I have a week off around Christmas?

Boss: It's May.

Man: Sorry. May I have a week off around Christmas?

I had a pet newt once. I called him Tiny...

Because he was my newt.

My girlfriend left a note on the fridge saying: "This isn't working. I'm leaving."

What a liar! I opened the fridge door and it's working fine.

———

Breaking news: An Italian branch of Heinz Soups has just gone into administrone!

What's a goblin's favourite dinner?

Ghoulash.

---

A thief tried to steal the paintings at the Louvre in Paris.

He was caught two streets away when he ran out of petrol.

He said, "I had no Monet to buy Degas to make the Van Gogh. But I tried because I had nothing Toulouse."

I was at a job interview today when the manager handed me a laptop and said, "I want you to try to sell this to me."

So I put it under my arm, left the building and went home.

Eventually he called me and said, "Bring my laptop back now."

I said, "£200 and it's yours."

———

I showed my badly damaged luggage to a lawyer and said, "I want to sue the airline."

He said, "But you don't have much of a case."

My friend said he didn't understand what cloning was.

I said that makes two of us.

———————

I spent ten minutes trying to remember what the opposite of "night" was.

In the end I had to call it a day...

If Bill Gates had a penny for every time he reboots my computer...

Oh wait...he does.

---

"Welcome back everybody" is apparently not a good way to start a speech..if you're the best man at your friend's second wedding.

I just made sure my daughter inherits
our bathroom scales after I die.

Because where there's a will
there's a weigh.

———————

Why did the whale cross the ocean?

To get to the other tide.

My girlfriend asked, "How do you feel about getting married?"

I replied, "It has a nice ring to it."

———————

Husband: I've looked everywhere and I can't find it.

Translation: I looked in one spot and gave up because I'm lost without you.

**Why were the two crows arrested?**

**Murder.**

---

**I didn't eat anything other than brown bread for dinner.**

**That was my wholemeal.**

# What do you call an ancient Egyptian?

# An old Giza.

My wife has kicked me out because of my bad Arnold Scharzenegger impressions. Don't worry...

...I'll return.

---

I once tried to show off to a girl by telling her I had made a car entirely from spaghetti.

She said she could never be with someone who made up such stupid lies.

You should have seen her face when I drove straight pasta!

I looked longingly into my beloved's eyes and whispered, "A...E...I...O...U and sometimes Y."

The priest turned to her and said, "And has the bride prepared any wedding vowels?"

---

I just found out I'm colour blind.

The diagnosis came out of the purple.

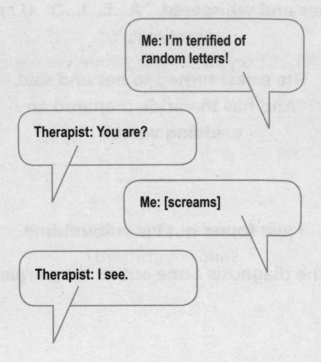

**What do you call a beehive without an exit?**

**Unbelievable.**

---

**What happens if you throw a Finnish sailor overboard?**

**Helsinki.**

My wife said she saw a bow tie made of solid mahogany. She said she nearly bought it for me but she didn't think I'd wear it.

I replied: "Wooden tie?"

---

I ordered a giant duck at a fancy restaurant last night.

The bill was huge!

I saw my ex-wife across the museum hall, but I felt too self-conscious to say hello.

There was just too much history between us.

———

How do you make an egg roll?

Push it downhill.

What's the one thing to guarantee you get butterflies?

Caterpillar.

I yelled "Cow!" to a women on a bike and she gave me the finger.

Then she rode straight into the cow.

———————

What did the green grape say to the purple grape?

OMG!!!!!!BREATHE!!!!!!!!!!BREATHE!!!!!

**What did the policeman say to his belly button?**

**You're under a vest.**

_____

**Why is 16 always full?**

**Because it 8 and 8.**

A ship carrying red paint collided with a ship carrying blue paint.

Both crews ended up marooned.

_____

Why do the Swedish navy have bar codes on their ships?

So when they return to port they can Scandinavian.

**What do you call two worms in love?**

**Soilmates.**

———————

**Recently I bumped into the guy who sold me my antique globe.**

**It's a small world.**

Someone dropped a power tool on my head the other day.

One minute I was fine, then BOSCH!

---

My favourite word is drool.

It just rolls off the tongue.

**Why can't Stevie Wonder see his friends?**

**Because he's married.**

---

**Whoever lost their phone outside the bar.**

**Please stop ringing my new phone.**

It wasn't much fun when I broke my neck last year.

But now I can look back and laugh.

------------

True fact:

before the crowbar was invented most crows drank at home.

I've been prescribed anti-gloating cream.

I can't wait to rub it in.

———————

Spring is here, but I can't plant
flowers yet...

I haven't botany.

Why do cows wear bells around their necks?

Because their horns don't work.

I just came home from work when my wife ran towards me and tore off all her clothes.

At that point, my wife flashed before my eyes.

———————

Don't you hate it when people answer their own questions?

I do.

Wife: I need an anagram for "nuclear".

Me: That's unclear.

My husband always buys cheap toilet paper...

It's a pain in the arse.

_____

My friend keeps saying, "Cheer up, it could be worse, you could be in a hole in the ground full of water."

I know he means well.

**What do you call a tired skeleton?**

**The Grim Sleeper.**

———————

**I've never seen the inside of my ears...**

**But I've heard good things.**

Just spent £300 on a limousine and discovered that the fee doesn't include a driver.

Can't believe I've spent all that money and have nothing to chauffeur it.

———

My wife and I were up all night arguing about the laundry.

At 2am, I folded.

Arguing with my wife is like reading a software licence agreement?

In the end I ignore it all and click "I agree."

———————

At the Olympics I saw an athlete carrying a long stick and asked him, "Are you a pole vaulter?"

He replied, "No, I'm German, but how do you know my name is Walter?"

What is green and sings?

Elvis Parsley.

You hear about the latest book on poltergeists?

It's flying off the shelves.

———

I finally bought my daughter her first watch.

It's about time.

My girlfriend poked my in the eyes...

so I stopped seeing her for a while.

_____

Why do the French only use one egg when baking a cake?

Because one egg is un oeuf.

Mark Knopfler and Chris Rea have formed a new band.

It's called Dire Rea.

------

Why do all beaches smell of urine?

Because the sea wee'd.

I just got the job as the senior director of the Old MacDonald farm.

I'm now the CIEIO.

----------

My son wanted to know what it's like to be married.

I asked him to leave me alone and when he did I asked him why he was ignoring me.

**How do you invite a dinosaur for lunch?**

**Tea, Rex?**

---

**If two witches watched two watches,
which witch would watch which watch?**

**Each witch would watch which watch
belonged to which witch's wrist.**

Where did Noah keep his bees?

In his Ark hives.

———————

My wife bought me a hideous leather jacket, but I don't mind wearing it.

I'm easily suede.

I told my dad I want to see *Spider-Man: Far From Home*.

He said, "But surely it's the same movie if you watch it here."

---

I've dedicated my whole life to finding a cure for insomnia.

I won't rest until I find it.

I didn't think vodka
could help
my problems.

But it was worth
a shot.

My wife told me she thought we'd have less arguments if I wasn't so pedantic.

I told her, "I think you mean fewer."

———————

What do farmers give to their wives on Valentine's Day?

Hogs and kisses.

My weird boss has assigned designated toilet breaks for all employees – and now it's my turn.

I really don't need this shit!

————————

The gluteus maximus is the largest muscle in your body,

In fact, it's a huge ass muscle.

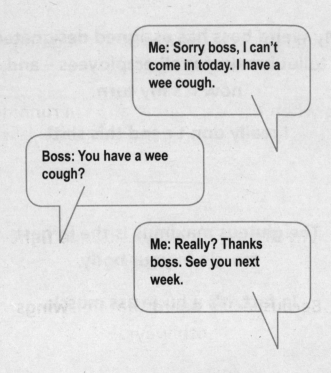

When I become a superhero I'm going to be called "Ironic".

So when there's trouble and I'm running away they'll shout, "Isn't that ironic?"

———————

Why did the monkey and Jane fight over Tarzan?

Because they heard that he swings both ways.

I used to be in a band called Missing Cat.

You probably saw our posters.

_____

My doctor told me to drink two glasses of red wine after a hot bath...

But I can't even finish drinking the hot bath.

If your can opener can't open a particular can, it becomes a cannot opener.

———————

Which days of the week are the strongest?

Saturdays and Sundays. The rest are weekdays.

So far, Humpty Dumpty is having a terrible winter.

Which sucks because he had a great fall.

My wife has this weird OCD where she arranges the dinner plates by the date they were bought.

It's an extremely rare dish order.

———

My wife asked if she could have some peace and quiet while she tried to cook dinner.

So I took the batteries out of the smoke alarm.

People say that circumcision doesn't hurt, but I disagree.

I was circumcised when I was born and I couldn't walk for over a year.

_____

What is the root of all evil?

25.8069758011

**A man goes to the doctor for a physical...**

Patient: Don't be alarmed but I have five penises.

Doctor: Five penises? How do your trousers fit?

Patient: Like a glove.

My girlfriend said to me, "I know you've been cheating on me with that girl from Llanfairpwllgwyngyllgogerychwyrndrob-wllllantysiliogogogoch."

I said, "How can you say such a thing?"

———————

Did you hear about the ventriloquist whose dummy is a donkey?

He's always talking out of his ass.

**What did the baby corn say to the momma corn?**

**Where is pop corn?**

_____

**My wife always wanted a son with a foreign-sounding name, so after she gave birth she decided on Mark but with a "C".**

**I just went to register his name now I'm so excited to get home to see little baby Cark!**

What do you call a deceased
Finnish man?

Finnished.

_____

I'm never again donating money to
anyone collecting for a marathon.

They just take the money and run.

Doctor: Sorry about your wait.

Patient: I am too, but I've been fat all my life.

Two drunk guys were about to get into a fight. One draws a line in the dirt and says, "If you cross this line, I'll hit you in the face."

That was the punchline.

_____

Asked my date to meet me at the gym, but she never showed up.

Guess the two of us aren't going to work out.

I dowloaded the
soundtrack
to *Titanic.*

It's syncing now.

What's Russia favourite
streaming platform?

Nyetflix.

———————

Why didn't the skeleton want to send
any Valentine's Day cards?

His heart wasn't in it.

**What do you get when you mix a motorcycle with a joke?**

**A Yamahaha.**

---

**What do you call a boomerang that doesn't come back?**

**A stick.**

Wouldn't it have been amazing if John Lennon had invented that device that you put in your front door to secretly see who's on the other side?

Imagine all the peepholes.

---

What did the octopus say to his girlfriend when he proposed?

Can I have your hand, hand, hand, hand, hand, hand, hand, hand in marriage?

**What did the French chef give his wife for Valentine's Day?**

**A hug and a quiche!**

———————

**A termite walks into a bar and asks:**

**"Is the bar tender here?"**

How do you put a baby astronaut to sleep?

You rocket.

———————

Spiders are the only web developers who love finding bugs.

For Valentine's Day I would have bought flowers for my girlfriend...

But my wife won't let me.

_____

Gambling addiction hotlines would do so much better...

If every fifth caller was a winner.

What do you call a polite person who builds bridges?

A civil engineer.

Bilbo awoke one morning to find that a supermarket had been built next to his house.

There's an unexpected item in the Baggins area.

———————

I don't want to brag, but I finished the jigsaw puzzle in a week and it said 2–4 years on the box.

Sometimes I wake up grumpy.

But other times I let him sleep in.

———————

My son just accused me of lying.

I wouldn't mind but I don't even have any children.

I broke my finger today.

But on the other hand I'm fine.

———————

Why do elephants hate running on
the beach?

Because they can't keep their trunks up.

I made my son some scrambled eggs and as he was eating them I turned to him and asked, "Are they all they were cracked up to be?"

---

When she heard me sing, my music teacher told me I should be tenor.

Tenor twelve feet away from every musical instrument.

I was explaining to my son how a baton is used in relay races and he understood right away.

I gotta hand it to him.

---

Today I saw an ad that said: Radio for sale, £1, volume is stuck at max level.

I thought, I just can't turn that down.

**Wife: I just got stung by a jellyfish. Quick, pee on it.**

**Husband: (peeing on jelly fish)That's for stinging my wife!**

Turned 18 today, so I bought a locket and put my own picture in it. Guess I really am...

Independent.

---

I've just finished reading a book called, *How to Avoid Getting Ripped Off.*

Best £100 I ever spent!

I went to a psychic and knocked on her front door. She yelled "who is it?".

So I left.

---

I told my wife I wanted cremated.

She made an appointment for Tuesday.

What do you call a nut with facial hair?

A mustachio.

How many tropical birds does it take to screw in a light bulb?

Two-can.

---

What do you call a teacher who doesn't fart in public?

A private toot-er.

What is the medical diagnosis for owning too many dogs?

Roverdose.

---

Why are French snails the fastest in the world?

L'ess cargo.

My friend told me that he got a new job testing athletes for doping at the next Olympics.

I think he's just taking the piss.

———————

My son was spending too much time playing computer games, so I said, "Son, when Abe Lincoln was your age, he was studying books by the light of the fire."

He considered this for a moment and replied, "When Abe Lincoln was your age he was the President of the United States."

Two windmills are standing in a field. Wanting to pass the time in conversation, one turns to the other and asks, "What kind of music do you like?"

The second turns and says, "I'm a big metal fan."

---

What do you call a bigoted fashion designer?

Clothes-minded.

Where does a tongue go to drop off its old clothes?

The Salivation Army.

_____

My wife is fed up of my constant word play jokes, so I asked her, "How can I stop my addiction?"

"Whatever means necessary," she replied.

"No it doesn't," I said.

I slapped Dwayne Johnson's ass.

Didn't feel like it at the time, but I realized I had hit rock bottom.

———————

For years I was against
organ transplants.

Then I had a change of heart.

# How do you get a farm girl to like you?

# A tractor.

I believe a lot of conflict in the
Wild West could have been
avoided completely...

...if cowboy architects had just made the
towns big enough for everyone.

———————

I have a Russian friend who's a
sound technician.

And a Czech one too. A Czech one too.

My boss told me that as a security guard, it's my job to watch the office.

I'm on the second series, but I'm not really sure what it's got to do with security.

———————

My wife said I should try lunges to stay in shape.

That would be a big step forward for me.

Which is heavier, the collected works of Shakespeare or a prison full of inmates?

The prose outweighs the cons.

———————

I got a bar installed into my roof.

Just so whenever I have guests I can say, "Drinks are on the house."

**What do you call a red-headed baker?**

**A gingerbread man.**

———————

**In which Indian city do people always leave their mothers?**

**Mumbai.**

**What smells better than it tastes?**

**A nose.**

_____

**Why did the two worms have to leave their apple to get into Noah's Ark?**

**Because they could only go in pears.**

Why is "Dark" spelled with a "K", and not a "C"?

Because you can't C in the dark.

_____

My wife's leaving me because she thinks I'm obsessed with astronomy.

What planet is she on?

Two friends chat and one boasts about his new car...

Friend 1: So I've got a new Tesla Model X; it drives itself.

Friend 2: Nice...where is it?

Friend 1: No Idea!

I'm an optimistic pessimist.

I'm positive things will go wrong.

———————

My friend is obsessed with taking blurry pictures of himself while taking a shower.

He has serious selfie steam issues.

I don't trust stairs.

They're always up
to something.

My boss at Pixar and I got into a fight over our lack of new movies.

But then we made *Up*.

---

Why did the S&M addict give up using his cat o' nine tails?

He was at his whips-end!

The internet connection at my farm is really sketchy, so I moved the modem to the barn.

Now I have stable WiFi.

———————

My wife asked me, "What starts with F and ends in K."

I said, "No it doesn't."

Why did the rapper get gold teeth?

He wanted to put his money where his mouth is.

————————

My dad died last year when my family couldn't remember his blood type for the blood transfusion.

As he was dying he kept on saying "be positive", but it's very hard without him.

I couldn't find my car scraper this morning so I had to use a store discount card to scrape the ice.

It didn't really work though, I only got 20% off.

---

You know, my hen counts her own eggs...

...she's a mathemachicken.

There was a big moron and a little moron sitting on a fence. The big moron fell off. Why?

The little moron was a little more on.

———————

My wife says I have two faults.

I don't listen...and something else.

**David Hasselhoff walked into a bar and ordered a drink...**

Bartender: It's a pleasure to serve you Mr Hasselhoff.

David Hasselhoff: Just call me Hoff.

Bartender: Sure, no hassle.

Not to brag, but I have this incredible talent for predicting what's inside a wrapped present.

It's a gift.

_____

Indian takeaway – £20

Cost of delivery – £2

Getting home to find out they've forgotten part of your order?

Riceless.

# Don't use double negatives.

# They're a big no no.

**Husband: I need to call the doctor today.**

**Wife: Which doctor?**

**Husband: No, the regular kind.**

Once my dog ate all the Scrabble tiles.

For days he kept leaving little messages around the house.

———

Did you hear about the actor who fell through the floorboards?

He was just going through a stage.

I waited and stayed up all night and tried to figure out where the sun was.

Then it dawned on me.

———————

As a scarecrow, people say I'm outstanding in my field.

But, hay, it's in my jeans.

Scientists have just discovered a fossilized dinosaur fart.

They say it's a blast from the past.

———————

I can't believe I was arrested for impersonating a politician.

I was just sitting around doing nothing.

Teacher: I wished you would pay a little attention.

Pupil: I'm paying as little as I can!

Long ago, my grandfather used to make huge holes on his land, so that they could hold water.

Once a pond a time.

———————

I keep having this dream about a horse in full battle armour.

Actually it's more of a knight mare.

I'm really upset!
Someone stole my
limbo stick!

I mean, how low
can you go?

**What does Arnold Schwarzenegger say at the beginning of a game of chess?**

**"I'll be black."**

_____

**Today someone told me I am average.**

**I told them that's just mean.**

**Dr: I'm afraid your DNA is backwards.**

**Me: And?**

———————————

**Why do some people post long jokes here?**

**This isn't where they be long.**

My dad always said "The first rule of theatre is to always leave them wanting more."

Great bloke.

Terrible anaesthetist.

———

An oracle once told me it was fate that I had banged my leg into a table at school.

I guess it was my desk to knee.

My friend asked me, "What's the best part about living in Switzerland?"

I said, "I don't know, but the flag is a big plus."

————————

My dad told me that when he was young, he once had to miss class because of hypothermia.

Said he was too cool for school.

A guy goes into a lawyer's office and asks...

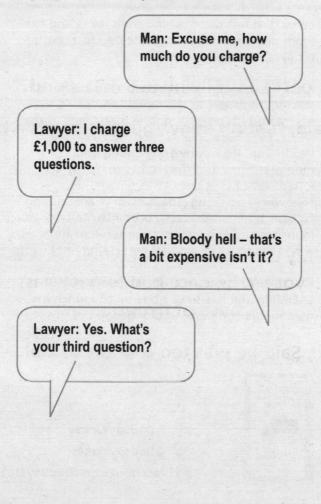

@DadSaysJokes is a community-run social brand with over 1 million followers on Instagram and Facebook, inspired by the daily jokes of author Kit Chilvers' dad, Andrew.

Every day, followers submit their jokes and the team pick their favourites – or Dad just drops in his own zinger!

Kit, a 19-year-old social networking mastermind started his career at the tender age of 14, when he created his original online platform, Football. Newz, to serve audiences for the 2014 FIFA World Cup. He has recently added another nine platforms in different genres (of which @DadSaysJokes is one), with nine million followers and rising. The networks are helping to launch new music acts, promote major product launches and live stream from some of the world's biggest sports and entertainment events.

Kit started his career at social media publisher LADBible and has since gone on to launch his own media company, Pubity Group Ltd.

**Also available:**

:camera: **@DadSaysJokes**

:bird: **@Dadsaysjokes**

:f: **facebook.com/DadSaysJokes**